IS MY PHONE READING MY MIND?

DR MATT AGNEW

ALLEN&UNWIN
SYDNEY·MELBOURNE·AUCKLAND·LONDON

First published by Allen & Unwin in 2024

Allen & Unwin
Cammeraygal Country
83 Alexander Street
Crows Nest NSW 2065
Australia
Phone: (61 2) 8425 0100
Email: info@allenandunwin.com
Web: www.allenandunwin.com

Allen & Unwin acknowledges the Traditional Owners of the Country on which we live and work.
We pay our respects to all Aboriginal and Torres Strait Islander Elders, past and present.

 A catalogue record for this book is available from the National Library of Australia

ISBN 978 1 76118 044 6

For teaching resources, explore allenandunwin.com/learn

Cover design and illustration by Astred Hicks, Design Cherry
Author photo by Wes Nel
Text design by Sandra Nobes
Internal illustrations by Hana Kinoshita Thomson
Robot illustrations throughout are inspired by Honda's ASIMO robot, p21: Shutterstock / DenisKlimov
Gorilla and kitten, p13: Shutterstock / David Carillet
Set in 12 pt Neutra Text Book Alt
This book was printed in March 2024 in China by 1010 Printing Limited

10 9 8 7 6 5 4 3 2 1

drmattagnew.com

CONTENTS

INTRODUCTION

Hi there! Fancy meeting you in a place like this! I'm **Dr Matt**, and I'm beyond excited that you're reading this book! Maybe you picked it up because you're like me and have a love of all things robotic? Maybe it was because you're keen on anything to do with science, and this book jumped out at you? Or maybe it was the fabulous front cover that drew you in? Whatever it was, **I'm delighted you're here!**

I love robots! I've always loved robots. I think we all have a bit of a robot phase as kids, and sometimes (if we're lucky) that sticks around well into our adult lives. I was fortunate enough to eventually study and work within the world of **artificial intelligence** (not the *actual* robots, more the 'brain' that could eventually direct robots). By being involved in this exciting world, I learned a lot about not just how it works, but also, and maybe more importantly, how it can influence us in interesting and unknown ways. But I'm getting ahead of myself.

Welcome to our journey to understanding artificial intelligence and its ethics! There are several words in that sentence that we need to define, and don't you worry – we will! We'll walk through things slowly until you can call yourself an **artificial intelligence ethics expert** (try saying that three times fast!).

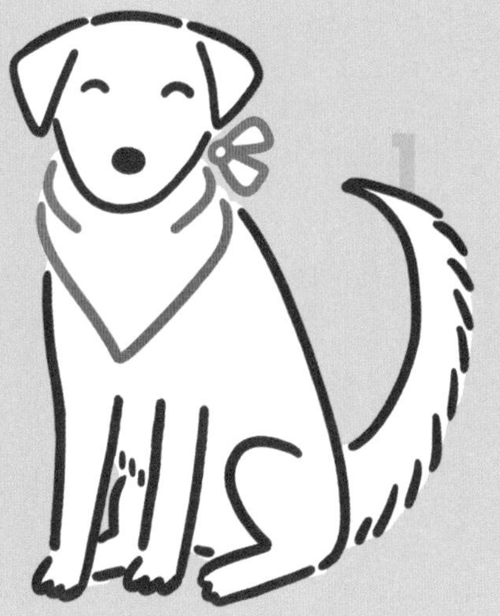

Artificial intelligence is all around us. It is becoming a **bigger** and **more important** part of our lives every day. While you don't necessarily need to know *how* all the clever artificial intelligence around you works (it's very complex!), it is important to know that it *does* exist, and that it is influencing your life, maybe in ways you didn't even realise!

And with the increase of artificial intelligence in your life, we need to ask questions. **How much should we trust artificial intelligence? Is it looking out for us? How do we know it isn't making us think in certain ways?** The answers to these questions are important so that we can live in harmony with artificial intelligence, and so that we continue to be in control of our lives and our thinking.

On our journey to understanding the ethics of artificial intelligence, we'll start with the basics. **First things first!**

FUN BUBBLE!

Welcome to the Fun Bubble! Throughout this book, I'll keep things interesting by having plenty of these little bubbles of fun. Inside each might be a little fun fact, cool story or just a surprising detail about the topic we are covering.

So, feel free to read these as they pop up, skip over them if you're in a good reading rhythm, or come back at the end of each chapter to read them one after the other. It's completely up to you!

BRAIN BOX

Sometimes you might come across a word you're unsure about. Never fear - the BRAIN BOX is here to explain what it means!

It's a nice reminder that none of us know all the answers, and we should never feel scared to ask for help. I certainly ask a lot of questions when I don't know something!

We'll go through exactly what artificial intelligence is, and where we can find it in our everyday lives. Then we can dive into the big and important stuff: the ethics of artificial intelligence. We'll look at how our own views of the world can influence how artificial intelligence works, how artificial intelligence can be misused, the impact artificial intelligence will have on humans as it continues to develop, and finally how we might best control artificial intelligence as we go hurtling into the future.

After you finish reading this book, I hope you'll walk away armed with new knowledge about artificial intelligence and ethics, what steps we must take to keep us all **safe**, and how artificial intelligence can **shape** and **enrich** our world.

FIRST THINGS FIRST

PART ONE

CHAPTER I:
WHAT IS ARTIFICIAL INTELLIGENCE?

The obvious starting point: just what exactly is artificial intelligence (or AI)? Well, let's look at each word by itself, then figure out what happens when we combine them.

What does ARTIFICIAL mean?

Artificial has a nice and easy definition: it was **built by humans.** This is different from things that occur naturally – a flower, for example. Nature creates flowers – we don't build them.

However, compare a flower to, say, a computer. A computer is artificial. A computer doesn't grow out of the ground or hang from trees. We (humans) build them. So **artificial** means that **we've built it**.

What does INTELLIGENCE mean?

Intelligence is a little trickier to define. You and I are clearly intelligent. I wrote this book, and you are reading it, and understanding what I have written. It's obvious that **humans are intelligent**. We've invented cars, designed smartphones, explored the world, sent people to the Moon, discovered black holes, and built hugely complex and connected civilisations. All of these tasks require intelligence.

So, we know we're intelligent. Compare ourselves to, say, plants. Trees don't build anything or have discussions amongst themselves. Nor do flowers, vegetables or fruits. In fact, anything that could be considered a plant clearly doesn't demonstrate intelligent behaviour.

You might ask, 'But what about sunflowers that turn to face the sun? Or Venus flytraps that capture flies?' There's a very small difference here: these actions happen as a response when some **trigger** fires, a bit like the bang from a starting pistol that signals to everyone to start running a race. That bang (or trigger) is called a **stimulus**.

A sunflower turns to face the sun because it can detect where the light is coming from – therefore, the sunlight is the stimulus that the flower is reacting to. It's not deciding, 'Hey, there's the sun, I'll just point myself that way!' The flower has been created by nature and has evolved to have a better chance of survival the more sun it gets, so it responds by turning to face the sun.

It's the same situation with the Venus flytrap responding to the stimulus of a fly landing. The Venus flytrap is not making cunning plans to capture its prey; it's just automatically responding to the stimulus by closing its 'mouth' around the fly. And it's not even an actual mouth – just a clever mechanism consisting of two hinged lobes.

Okay, so we know what is **definitely intelligent (us)** and what is **definitely *not* intelligent (plants),** but between these extremes, what happens? There must be some cut-off point or boundary where things are either intelligent or not. **But where is that line?**

Let's try to work down from the intelligent side. Are the other great apes (gorillas, orang-utans, and chimpanzees) intelligent? Watch them socialise at the zoo – it's obvious **they're also intelligent.** In fact, they're so intelligent that

CHEEKY KOKO

Koko the gorilla captured the hearts of millions of people, especially those who met her. She learned to use over 1000 signs and could understand around 2000 words in spoken English. Koko made a huge impact on our understanding of the intelligence of primates (the class of animals that we humans belong to, along with other great apes and monkey-like animals).

Koko was allowed to adopt a kitten, All Ball, as a companion. One day, Koko was misbehaving, and tore a steel sink from the wall. In a clear display of intelligence, she tried to blame All Ball, signing 'cat did it'. Obviously no one believed Koko, but it was certainly a bit of a 'wow' moment as she demonstrated the ability to lie.

one gorilla, Koko, was taught sign language to communicate with humans.

Well then, what about dogs? The fact you can teach a dog commands should make it obvious **they're also intelligent.** Just watch any working dog perform its duties, and it's even more obvious!

This is getting hard! How about we try working up from the **not intelligent** end instead?

Bacteria? Scientists have studied **bacterial intelligence**, but they're definitely not making plans, solving problems, or learning in the same way we (or even dogs) are. **What about coral?** It certainly doesn't appear intelligent in the same way we do. It seems to behave more like plants.

Okay, so it's difficult from the **non**-intelligent side too. What do we do?

It's certainly a tricky problem to answer, especially when we consider there are 'levels' of intelligence. We are smarter than the other great apes. The other great apes are smarter than dogs. Dogs are smarter than fish, and so on. **So where do we draw that line?**

For this discussion, let's use one imperfect yet easy definition: **intelligence is the ability to solve problems.**

So, let's put these two definitions together: **artificial intelligence is something built by humans that can solve problems.**

That wasn't so bad, right? And now we have a good, clean definition of just what exactly AI is. **Lovely!**

Having said that, we still need to think a little bit when classifying things. **Is a calculator AI?** Humans certainly built it (we're not going out to pick calculators off the calculator tree), and it solves problems – it sounds like AI. The difference is that *we* have to operate it. It's a **tool** that we use.

The same is true for computers. Humans have definitely built them, and they're definitely used to solve problems, but again, we're operating them. They're very **clever tools**, but they're still tools.

So, what are actual examples of AI? We'll get to that in Chapter 2, so let's first discuss an important part of AI – and a word you may have come across before.

What is an ALGORITHM?

Simply put, algorithms are the **lifeblood of artificial intelligence.**

You see, the thing about artificial intelligence is that it's not necessarily how we think of it in science fiction stories. AI is not limited to walking, talking robots that we interact with. AI can be much simpler, yet still fit our definition of **something built by humans that can solve problems.**

It could be something as simple as the spelling and grammar check when you're typing out a story or assignment for school; something a little cleverer, like the way a map app in your parents' car or on their phone gives you directions; or even something a bit more 'magical' like YouTube or your favourite streaming service predicting what you sort of things you like watching by recommending similar shows or movies to you. We can use clever artificial intelligence algorithms to do all these things. But even for really clever, advanced AI that *does* interact with humans, there is a challenge that we haven't yet figured out.

The **challenge** is that there are parts of intelligence that we still don't fully understand. **Consciousness** is perhaps the biggest mystery.

What this means is that even when interacting with the most advanced AI we have ever built - even if it *feels* like we're talking to a smart, thinking robot - we are still interacting with a bunch of clever algorithms that create the illusion of **consciousness.**

However, in both these scenarios (simple AI programs and clever, advanced, interactive AI) and everything in between, it is **the algorithm that makes the AI work**. So enough about why it's important - just what is it?

CONSCIOUSNESS is very hard to define perfectly, but a simple definition is the ability to feel, experience, perceive and be aware of one's surroundings, and the ability to understand these things internally with our thoughts.

We don't really know how it works, and we certainly don't know how to build or program consciousness.

THE TURING TEST

The Turing test (named after Alan Turing, who paved the way for artificial intelligence) is a test to decide if an AI is intelligent. The basic idea is this: imagine you have two chat programs open. One chat program is being operated by a human, and the other by an AI. If you can't figure out which is which, the AI is said to have passed the Turing test. It's so good you don't know whether you're talking to a human or an AI!

At its simplest, **an algorithm is a** **recipe.** It is a series of steps or instructions that - when followed - will produce a result. For example, here's an algorithm for baking brownies:

1. Position an oven rack in the middle of the oven. Preheat the oven to 175° Celsius.

2. Line a 20 cm × 20 cm baking pan with baking paper or aluminium foil. Let the lining hang over the edges as handles (to help lift the brownies out later).

3. Mix 145 g melted butter in a bowl with 250 g white sugar, 80 g unsweetened cocoa and a pinch of salt.

4. Add a teaspoon of vanilla extract and mix well.

5. Crack 2 eggs into a cup before adding to bowl, and mix well.

6. Add 65 g plain flour to the bowl and mix well.

7. Spread the batter in a lined baking pan.

8. Bake for 20–30 minutes, then test with a toothpick in the centre. The brownies are ready when only a few moist crumbs stick to the toothpick.

9. Allow to cool completely before lifting out of pan with lining handles.

This is an algorithm that will produce a pan of brownies. If you're saying, 'But it's just a recipe,' you're right – an algorithm is essentially a recipe that computers perform.

One key difference, though, is an algorithm can also repeat the steps through instructions. Each time an algorithm repeats is called a **loop.** This means that an algorithm can be a series of instructions in a loop, and each time the loop is completed, the algorithm determines whether to stop or do another loop. For example, here's a set of instructions that loops for you eating a pizza:

1. Open pizza box.
2. Take slice of pizza.
3. Eat pizza slice.
4. a) If you are not full, go to step 2.
   b) If you are full or there are no more slices of pizza, go to step 5.
5. Close pizza box.

As you can see, you begin by opening the box, taking a slice, and eating the slice. The next instruction then depends on whether you're: a) not full, **or** b) full or there are no more slices. This is one of the clever parts of algorithms: that they can follow different paths depending on the answer to certain questions.

Algorithms get much more complex from here, but the key points are that they are a set of instructions, they can loop, and they can do different things depending on the answer to certain questions. This makes them very powerful, so you can see why **algorithms are the building blocks of all sorts of artificial intelligence.**

CHAPTER 2:
WHERE DO WE FIND AI IN OUR EVERYDAY LIVES?

So, we now know just what artificial intelligence is – but what we want to know next is how it affects us day to day. Just where are we seeing AI in our everyday lives?

If we think of AI as it appears in cartoons or sci-fi, it's often in the form of a **humanoid** (meaning *looks like a human*) robot that people interact with. Think about C-3PO in Star Wars, or the Autobots in Transformers. These sorts of robots are smart and can talk to humans, and they have been common in TV shows and movies for a long time. From the Terminator in, well, *The Terminator*, and the machines in *The Matrix* (ask your parents), to the Robot in *Lost in Space* and Rosey in *The Jetsons* (ask your grandparents), robots that humans can talk to and interact with have featured in popular culture for most of the past century.

This sort of AI – **a robot companion** – might help you with your homework, cook your food, clean the house, or do your mum and dad's gardening. It would definitely be a good example of AI, and

ROBO COMPANIONS

I know I said that we don't have robot companions yet – and we don't, really – but that doesn't mean that more and more businesses aren't working hard to develop robot companions that will help humans. One of the most well-known human-shaped robots is Honda's ASIMO.

ASIMO is able to walk on two legs, and recognise moving objects, postures, gestures, sounds, faces and its environment. Combining these abilities means ASIMO can interact with humans, *and* distinguish between different humans based on how they look or the sound of their voice.

So, maybe robotic companions are not very far away!

it is also very clear how it is impacting your life. However, we don't have such robot companions yet.

But this doesn't mean AI doesn't affect you. It just means that it affects you in different ways, and they are often invisible. To understand how AI affects our day-to-day lives, we need to learn a new term: **machine learning**.

Machine learning is a type of AI where humans design software or programs that **learn**, usually from something called **data**. Data is the scientific word for **information**. It could be words, numbers, pictures, or a combination of all three.

Some data about you might be your height (a **number**), your weight (a **number**), your hair colour (a **word**), your eye colour (a **word**), a photo of your face (a **picture**), or your fingerprint (a **picture**). Data, and how data is used, is becoming a bigger and more important part of our lives with every passing day, and one of the biggest ways data is being used is in machine learning algorithms. So, how does a machine learning algorithm work, and how is it being used to impact our lives?

A really simple application of machine learning could be predicting what breed a dog is if we only know the dog's weight. Imagine there are only two breeds of dogs: labradors and chihuahuas. Let's say you've got a pack of them.

With data, a machine can learn (or **be trained**) about this pack of dogs, such as the weight of a typical labrador or chihuahua. By giving this data to our machine for it to train with, we've made sure the machine has **learned** about these dogs - now if you told the machine the weight of a dog, it could predict whether the dog was a labrador or a chihuahua.

Let's explore this a little more. Look at this table of data of our pack of dogs:

DOG BREED	WEIGHT (KG)
Labrador	29.0
Labrador	36.0
Chihuahua	1.8
Labrador	25.0
Chihuahua	2.0
Chihuahua	3.0
Labrador	27.5
Labrador	30.0
Chihuahua	2.1
Labrador	31.0

This small set of data (usually called a **dataset**) is where we start with machine learning. We train our machine learning algorithm on this dataset. The algorithm then begins to learn. Here's a visual of our pack of dogs dataset:

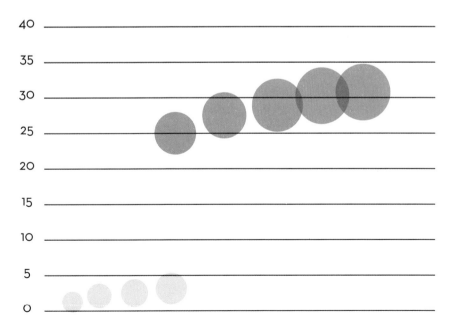

How the weight of ⬤ labradors and ⬤ chihuahuas differ

You can see that the two breeds have very obvious differences in weights, and we want our machine to realise this too. Let's use an algorithm that calculates the **average** weight of each dog breed and uses the averages to classify dogs based on weight. Now, before we jump too far ahead, we need to understand what an average is.

The average (let's use the commonly understood word *average* instead of the correct maths term, *mean*) of a group of numbers is the sum of those numbers, divided by how many numbers there are. It's sort of like the **'middle'** of the numbers.

As an example, imagine the group of numbers **2, 3, 4, 5** and **6**. How would we calculate the average? What we do is **add** up all the numbers and **divide** them by how many numbers there are. So, for our group of numbers we add them up to get:

$$2 + 3 + 4 + 5 + 6 = 20$$

And since there are 5 numbers in our group, we divide the total by 5 to get:

$$20 \div 5 = 4$$

So, the average of our group of numbers is 4. **Easy!**

You could do the same thing with weights. Imagine there are **5 dogs** with weights 12 kg, 3 kg, 24 kg, 26 kg, and 15 kg. Doing our calculations, we get:

$$12\,kg + 3\,kg + 24\,kg + 26\,kg + 15\,kg = 80\,kg$$

And since there are 5 numbers in this group too, we divide the total by 5 to get:

$$80\,kg \div 5 = 16\,kg$$

So, the average weight of these 5 dogs is 16 kg. Notice that none of our 5 dogs weigh 16 kg? The average isn't always a number in the group.

Okay, back to our pack of dogs. Our machine learning algorithm can learn the average weight of each breed of dog (often referred to as the *centroid* in such algorithms). We can then give our algorithm a dog weight as an input, and it will figure out which dog breed has an average weight that is 'closer' to this input value. Again, let's look at our dataset to better understand what 'closer' means.

The average weight for our two breeds from the data is:

DOG BREED	HOW MANY?	AVERAGE WEIGHT (KG)
Labrador	6	29.75
Chihuahua	4	2.225

Now, imagine if we told the machine learning algorithm that we have a dog that weighs 5 kg. Which dog breed would our algorithm predict?

We calculate the difference between the input number (5 kg) and the weights of the dogs (and always subtract the smaller number from the bigger number when we're calculating how 'close' two numbers are). For labradors, the **difference** is:

[average labrador weight] – [input number]
= [how close labradors are to input number]
29.75 kg – 5 kg = 24.75 kg

And for chihuahuas the **difference** is:

[input number] – [average chihuahua weight]
= [how close chiahuahuas are to input number]
5 kg – 2.225 kg = 2.775 kg

Since the difference between our input number and chihuahuas is smaller, the machine learning predicts that our 5 kg dog is probably a chihuahua.

Likewise, if we told the algorithm we have a dog that weighs 20 kg, our algorithm would predict that it is probably a labrador. Try the calculations above to see if this is correct – did you get the same answer as the algorithm?

This is an example of how a machine learning algorithm learns from a dataset and is then able to **predict** things for us.

MEANS AND MODES AND MEDIANS, OH MY!

As we mentioned above, the word *average* is said a lot when what we're actually talking about is the mathematical term *mean*. You see, an average is a single number that can describe or represent a group of numbers, and the mean is just one type of average. There are actually three types of averages that are commonly used:

The **MEAN**, which is what we explained earlier: when we add up all the numbers and divide them by how many numbers there are

The **MODE**, which is the most common number in a group of numbers

The **MEDIAN**, which is the middle number if you arranged the numbers from smallest to largest

Let's use an example. Say our group of numbers is:

7, 1, 8, 2, 5, 1, 6, 7, 3, 7, 8

We first calculate the mean. First, add all the numbers up:

$7+1+8+2+5+1+6+7+3+7+8=55$

And since there are 11 numbers, divide by 11:

$55 \div 11 = 5$

So, the mean is 5. What about the mode?

Let's count how many of each number there is:

NUMBER	HOW MANY?
1	2
2	1
3	1
5	1
6	1
7	3
8	2

We can see that the most common number is 7, so the mode is 7. What about the median? Let's arrange the numbers from smallest to largest:

1, 1, 2, 3, 5, 6, 7, 7, 7, 8, 8

Since there are 11 numbers, the middle number will be the one that is in the sixth position. In this case, that number is 6. Therefore, the median is 6.

So, while the mean (5), mode (7) and median (6) all differ, they are all useful in different ways and for different problems.

In reality, machine learning algorithms are much more complex, the way they use data to predict things is more complicated, and the sizes of their datasets are much bigger – in the millions or even billions of pieces of data. These big and clever algorithms are very powerful.

Our dog algorithm is all well and good, but we still haven't discovered the answer to the question: Where do we find AI in our everyday lives?

Chatterbox

The first example of AI in our everyday lives may not be the most common example (you might not use it or see it much) but when you do see it, it's arguably the most obvious! That is generative AI (it generates or creates something), and in particular ChatGPT.

ChatGPT is what is referred to as a Large Language Model (LLM) chatbot. LLMs are models that use tremendous amounts of written data to figure out the value of billions of little dials and sliders (known as parameters), by tweaking and changing the parameters as the model learns from all that data it is being fed. If that sounds confusing, it's because it is. LLMs are a type of algorithm called an artificial neural network which are a group of algorithms that are meant to mimic neurons in the brain. No wonder it's confusing – the way brains work *is* confusing!

IDEAS COME FROM CURIOSITY. OR AI.

ChatGPT is a tremendously powerful tool. The ability to input human-like text and get a response feels like magic. And it can do what one might consider 'creative' tasks, too.

Take this book, for example. We did loads of brainstorming and shortlisting and ended up with a fantastic title, but what if we had been really lazy and just wanted a snappy title without having to think about it? Well, we could have done that by giving a prompt like this to ChatGPT:

Dr Matt: Give me a list of 6 titles for a book about artificial intelligence for ages 8–12. Have half the list be serious titles, and the other half be silly titles.

ChatGPT: Certainly! Here's a list of book titles about artificial intelligence for ages 8–12, with a mix of serious and silly titles:

SERIOUS TITLES
1. *Journey into AI: Exploring the World of Artificial Intelligence*
2. *AI Adventures: Discovering the Secrets of Smart Machines*
3. *Tomorrow's Mind: The Future of Artificial Intelligence for Young Innovators*

SILLY TITLES
1. *Robots Ate My Homework: AI and Other Silly Stories*
2. *Giggle Bots: The Hilarious Side of Artificial Intelligence*
3. *Silly Circuits and Wacky Widgets: An AI Comedy for Kids*

These titles are designed to cater to the curiosity and imagination of children in that age group, with a balance of educational and fun, engaging storytelling.

The way ChatGPT works, though, is through being able to understand language in a very general sense. That is to say, you can talk to it and ask it to do things in normal, everyday language.

Type in a question and it'll reply in a nearly human-like way. Ask it to solve a problem for you and it'll have a go – and often be correct! Even ask it to give you ideas and it'll generate a list for you.

It can feel like you are talking to something very similar to an AI you'd see in a movie or a cartoon. It can be a bit eerie realising it's an algorithm you're talking to, but it's also **really, really** cool.

Video game warriors

There are some obvious examples of AI if you're into video games. If you play Minecraft, Fortnite or even just a chess game versus the computer, there are non-player characters (or **NPCs**) that will often have AI coded in. This is sometimes a simple 'rules-based' AI (a bit like our pizza-eating algorithm) which means it has a bunch of questions (known as **if statements**) that the AI checks to decide what to do:

- 👉 if A is true, then do B, otherwise
- 👉 if C is true, then do D, otherwise
- 👉 if E is true, then do F, otherwise
- 👉 ...

and so on for all the different things the NPC can do. The list of rules can be very long, and so quite complex AI can be created. As an example, think about how an AI playing a game of Monopoly might work. Imagine the AI has just rolled a die and landed on a property. It might go through the following logic to decide what to do:

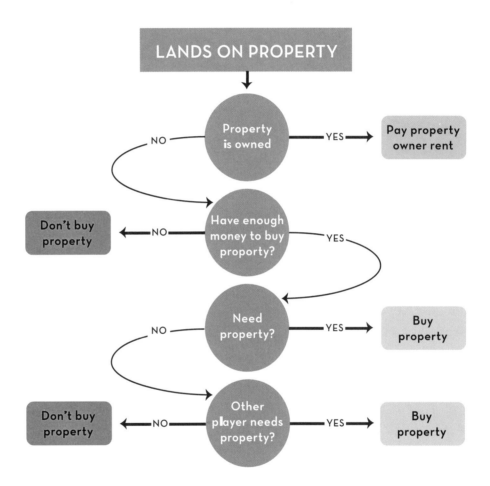

All of these steps individually are simple **yes/no** decisions, and the AI will do different things as a result of each. Put together, the AI makes decisions and performs actions when it lands on a property depending on a number of factors – similar to how we might make a decision.

THE
DEEPEST OF BLUES

AI learning to play computer games is nothing new. It's been done for a long time, and video games your parents played almost certainly had 'computer' opponents that they could play against or with, whether that's to race against in *Mario Kart*, to fight against in *Street Fighter*, or to nurture and blossom in *The Sims*.

Something that has also been done for a long time is to write software or programs that can compete with humans intellectually – much cleverer algorithms that people fine-tune over time to become better and better.

One of the most famous examples is Deep Blue, a chess-playing AI that ran on a supercomputer. In 1996 it faced off against Garry Kasparov, a chess grandmaster and World Chess Champion at the time. Kasparov beat Deep Blue, but after an upgrade a rematch was held in 1997. This time, Deep Blue defeated Kasparov, marking one of the most significant milestones in the history of artificial intelligence. AI was catching up to human intelligence (although in one very small application), and had defeated one of humanity's greatest intellects.

Some smooth selling

There are also some less obvious examples of AI. Have you or your parents ever ordered something on Amazon? Amazon can often deliver your order in only one day. But they can't possibly store their millions of products near every major city – there are just too many. So how does it work?

Machine learning is the answer. With millions (and even billions) of purchases over the years, a machine learning algorithm can learn how frequently a certain item is bought in a certain city. For example, the algorithm may learn that a particular frying pan is ordered roughly once a month in Adelaide, and twice a month in Melbourne. The frying pan is stored in the Melbourne warehouse. This means that when it is ordered in Melbourne it's close enough for a delivery the next day.

Now for the clever part! Since an order in Adelaide usually happens once a month, the machine learning algorithm tells Amazon to send a frying pan to Adelaide once a month **whether there is an order or not.** That way, when someone in Adelaide *does* order the frying pan, it is already in the warehouse.

It might sound like it is just guessing, and it sort of is, but it's a very educated guess because it has learned that there's a really high chance that someone will order a frying pan based on the millions of purchases before this one. You might ask, what if no one orders one? That's okay – the algorithm will take note of that and continue to improve its guessing ability. What about if more than one person orders one? It just means the second order will receive their frying pan slower. With a clever algorithm, this will be rare enough not to upset too many people!

How smart is that!? With enough data, we can **predict the future** – even if it's in very limited ways, such as whether or not someone is buying a frying pan! Of course, sometimes the algorithm will get it wrong. Humans aren't clocks or calendars – they don't do things at exactly the same time every month. But after millions or even billions of purchases, the algorithm has so much data that it gets better and better at guessing, so it is correct more often than it is wrong.

What do you want to watch?

Here's another example. Do you use a streaming service like Netflix? Maybe Disney+? Have you ever wondered how they give you the 'recommendations' they do? Similar to our dog pack, there is a clever machine learning algorithm that keeps track of what you watch. For example, it might follow these steps:

1. The algorithm collects all the movies and TV shows you've watched. It then looks at different properties (called features in machine learning) of the shows – the genre, how long the show is, the year it was made, the actors in it…the list goes on. It uses these details to create your 'profile'.

2. It finds other people who have watched many of the movies and TV shows that have features in common with those you have watched. This means these people have a similar profile to you – you both like the same kinds of shows.

3. It looks at all those people who have a similar profile as you and finds out what other movies and TV shows they have watched that you haven't watched.

4. It shows you those movies and TV shows as recommendations.

You may not be aware of it, but your streaming service's algorithm keeps track of what you're watching to make finding another show easier for you – rather than you having to look through the entire library to find something you'll enjoy. That sounds like a good thing, right?

However, this sort of tracking also happens with your internet searches, for example. The pages that show up for you, and the ads that pop up, are based on your search history and what other people with similar searches liked or clicked on. This can sound **creepy** – and maybe it is, a bit – but it's currently part of how our technology works.

This also extends to social media. If you have an Instagram or TikTok account (or maybe your older siblings or parents do), the algorithm that makes recommendations will also be tracking what you do. Not just what you like and comment on, but what videos you pause on, and for how long. Some of these apps also have buttons you can press that say things like 'Show me less of this' to directly tell the algorithm what you do and don't like.

For example, maybe you're not a big fan of sports, so you click on 'Show me less of this' to tell the algorithm to show you fewer sports clips; maybe you love cooking, so you tell the algorithm to 'Show me more of this' to see more cooking clips.

While you don't need to know exactly *how* the algorithm works, it's important to know that **it is happening.**

CHAPTER 3:
WHAT ARE ETHICS?

Where do we start when describing ethics? Are they the same as laws? How are they different?

At their simplest, **ethics** are the guidelines that help us understand if an action is right or wrong. Ethics can be applied to both an individual (for example, whether you personally should do something) or a larger entity (for example, whether a business should be doing something). There isn't just one set of ethics, but rather a number of different sets – and sometimes they can conflict and lead us to different decisions depending on which set we use.

So, what about **laws**? Laws have some similarities to ethics, but there are a few important differences. One is that laws are stronger than just being 'guidelines' – laws are rules that should not be broken. Breaking a law carries a consequence (sometimes ethics carry consequences too, but not always).

Another difference is that laws are written, published and maintained by an authority that enforces laws, such as the government. Ethics are less formal.

For example, you're in a supermarket and **really want a bar of chocolate**. You don't have any money, so perhaps you start wondering whether or not you should steal one. Your conscience tells you that you **shouldn't steal** - that it's the wrong thing to do. You decide not to steal.

So, how did ethics work here? Ethics help us to understand *why* stealing is the wrong thing to do. Ethics say you shouldn't steal because the chocolate bar doesn't belong to you, and you can't just steal other people's belongings (there's a little more to how we jump to this conclusion - we'll crack that open shortly). Ethics have helped your conscience decide what is right or wrong.

Okay, so ethics tell us not to steal a chocolate bar. Where do laws stand on stealing chocolate, then? It's quite simple: stealing is breaking the law. So, in this particular example, it turns out that both ethics and laws are in agreement. You shouldn't steal because the bar doesn't belong to you (ethics), and if you do steal then you're breaking the rules set by an authority (laws). Both terms indicate that you shouldn't steal.

Sometimes though, this isn't the case. For example, lying. Imagine a schoolmate is daydreaming in class, and later asks you if the teacher assigned any homework. Earlier that day they refused to trade a Pokémon card to you that you felt you deserved, as you'd helped them build their collection in the past. You're pretty grumpy with them, so as revenge, you decide to try to get them in trouble: you lie, 'No, we don't have any homework.' The next day, your teacher asks to see everyone's homework. The student you lied to is visibly upset and anxious, and sure enough, the teacher gives them a detention.

When you lied to them, you knew it would upset them and they would get in trouble. Ethically speaking, it is unkind and disrespectful to trick, deceive and inflict discomfort on someone like this, but you're not breaking the law. Ethics tell you not to lie, but the law doesn't punish you for lying (except in very specific cases).

What about eating meat? If you're not a vegetarian or vegan, and if you don't know anything about how meat is farmed, it probably doesn't feel wrong. If you *are* a vegetarian or vegan, though, you're likely to feel it's **very ethically wrong** to eat animals. What about laws, then? Well, it's certainly not illegal to eat meat (most meat, anyway). You see how messy things can get.

An important point to make about all this is that laws are applied to everyone equally, while ethics can vary person to person (maybe you don't see any problem with lying if the other person has done something that upset you), but also they can vary between what set of ethics one uses.

Sets of ethics

What do I mean when I say there are different sets of ethics? Well, what is **'right'** or **'wrong'** is not always clear. Take our lying example, where someone got in trouble because of your lie. **White lies**, on the other hand, are when you lie about something small that has no effect on anyone else. It might be just to make yourself look good – say you tell your friends about this cool trick you did on your bike. Your friends say how great you are, and it feels pretty good. But really, you made it up. You lied to your friends to make yourself look awesome. You haven't said anything to hurt someone else, though, so what's the harm?

WHITE LIES

Another example of a white lie is when you use them to spare someone's feelings. Imagine one of your friends is just getting into art. They're still learning, and they show you their first painting that they're really proud of. You don't think it looks very good. Should you tell them so?

You know being honest is important, and lying is almost always the wrong thing to do. But what are your options? The truth might hurt. You don't want to hurt your friend's feelings. Hurting our friends is almost always the wrong thing to do. So what then?

You might decide a white lie is the best option here. Rather than being totally honest and telling them it's really bad, maybe you say, 'You've done really well. Great effort!' It's not a good habit to lie, but sometimes it can be kind to bend the truth so you don't hurt your friend's feelings.

It will depend on how we decide what is right or wrong. Is the act of lying considered wrong no matter what? Or because the white lie is harmless, is it considered right? The answer depends on which guidelines we use.

Different sets of ethics have different guidelines. Let's discuss two sets of ethics here: **Kantian** ethics and Utilitarian ethics.

There's a number of aspects to Kantian ethics, but for our purposes the main idea is:

Act in a way in which you would be happy for everyone to act.

Think about this in terms of the chocolate bar example. Should you steal the chocolate bar? Well, let's say we're happy for everyone to steal chocolate bars. What would that look like?

It would be chaos! Your chocolate bar would likely be stolen immediately after you'd stolen it yourself. So you could steal another, but that bar would probably be taken too. You go to steal a third - but the shop no longer has any because they've all been stolen. So you'd have to turn to stealing from other people instead.

It would become a wild chocolate-stealing frenzy! It wouldn't work. People would be hungry for chocolate, then

KANTIAN ETHICS are named after Immanuel Kant, a German philosopher (1724-1804). He made huge contributions to the world of philosophy, so much so that he is sometimes called the 'father of modern philosophy'.

be angry when it all goes wrong, maybe some would turn violent…Not a good idea at all! So Kantian ethics tell us not to steal the chocolate bar.

The other set of ethics we'll look at is Utilitarian ethics. These are much simpler to understand:

Act in a way that produces the greatest good for the greatest number of people.

This means that the ethics around the chocolate-stealing are a little different. Utilitarian ethics don't necessarily see stealing the chocolate bar as right or wrong. If you steal you are happy, while the shopkeeper is sad. The good balances out the bad.

However, with a few more details that outcome can change. Instead of stealing the chocolate bar for yourself, imagine you are actually stealing it to share between you and a friend. Now, while stealing is bad for the shopkeeper, it is good for you *and* your friend. In this scenario, stealing **maximises the good**: 1 person is still sad, but now 2 people are happy. In this situation, Utilitarian ethics say that stealing is the 'right' thing to do.

Let's try adding another detail. Imagine now that there are 10 people who co-own the shop, though only 1 of them is ever working at a time. Now, stealing the chocolate bar

There are many UTILITARIAN ETHICISTS, and one of the most well known is Jeremy Bentham (1747-1832), often regarded as the founder of modern Utilitarianism. Bentham led a remarkable life, and his death is just as memorable. As per his wishes, his skeleton and head were preserved, and can sometimes be found on display at the University College London – a university he helped establish in 1826.

means the shop loses money, which means all 10 people have lost a little bit of money. While you and your friend are happy, there are now 10 other people who are sad about having a chocolate bar stolen. Now Utilitarian ethics tell us that stealing is the 'wrong' thing to do.

You can see how applying ethics can give different results depending on what set is used, and the circumstances they are being used in. For practice, let's apply Kantian and Utilitarian ethics to a well-known ethical thought experiment: **the tram problem**.

The tram problem

The tram problem, more commonly known as **the Trolley Problem** (don't panic – it doesn't have anything to do with supermarket trolleys! In the USA, a trolley is actually a tram), is simple enough. Imagine a single tram track that forks into 2 tracks. On the left-hand track beyond the fork, 1 of your friends has been playing with their favourite toy and has left it there on the track. On the other, right-hand track, 5 of your friends have been playing with their favourite toys and have also left them on the second track.

A tram is coming along the single track, and the fork is set to lead right, to the 5 toys. That's disturbing enough, but here's the really tricky bit: *you* are in control of the lever to switch the track, which would re-direct the tram to the track with only 1 toy, saving 5 toys but destroying 1. What do you do?

It's not a pleasant scenario, but it shows how complex ethics are and why they are so important. If we apply Utilitarian ethics, you must pull the lever to switch the tracks. The greatest good is to keep as many people happy as possible, so you pull the lever - that way, you keep 5 friends happy by saving their toys, despite the fact your action will upset 1 person whose toy is sacrificed.

If we instead apply Kantian ethics, we get a different outcome. Remember, Kantian ethics ask us to consider if we would be happy if everyone acted in a certain way. So, the options are:

1. You pull the lever, which means you *have* acted, which means you have caused something.
2. You *don't* pull the lever, which means you *haven't* acted, which means you haven't caused something.

In the first option, the 'something' you have caused is the destruction of 1 person's toy for what you consider to be something 'good' (preserving 5 people's toys). Let's now imagine that everyone were to always decide to take an action to achieve something 'good', even if it meant destroying another person's toy.

Your own toy is broken? No problem! To make it good again you could just smash up someone else's toy to get the parts required to fix your own. Some classmate is building a science project that needs a motor? They should just crack your project in half to use the motor so they earn a good mark. Everyone breaking other people's things to achieve something 'good' doesn't sound like it would be very pleasant at all, does it?

With the second option, though, at least we haven't caused anything. Even though 5 toys will be destroyed, it is not because of our actions. So, Kantian ethics tell us to choose the second option: do *not* pull the lever.

GOTTA CATCH 'EM ALL

Here's an ethical dilemma for you. Imagine you're at school and it's recess. You're on your way to the oval to meet your friends when you notice a Pokémon card someone dropped on the ground. It's not just any Pokémon card, though; it's a Charizard – one of the rarest ones! It's in a little protective sleeve and the sleeve has a student's name written on it (presumably the owner of the card). You know this person is a bit of a bully, and maybe they deserve to be punished in some way. So, do you keep the rare Charizard card that you really *really* want (and punish the bully)? Or do you take it to the bully even though they're not very nice?

All this shows that there's no specific **'right'** or **'wrong'** answer to the tram problem. It helps us understand how different sets of ethics guide us to choose different actions. Kantian ethics tell us we should not pull the lever, while Utilitarian ethics tell us we should. When we first discussed the ethics, the guidelines of each sounded fair – but it turns out it is not so easy to understand the right or wrong thing to do in complicated scenarios.

Now that we know a little more about ethics, we can get into a new and exciting world full of artificial intelligence, algorithms and machine learning.

THE ETHICS OF AI

Alright! In **Part 1** we covered a lot of ground, so let's re-group for a moment! What do we now know? We've learned three key things:

1. what artificial intelligence is
2. where we might see AI in our day-to-day lives
3. what ethics are.

Fantastic! So, let's combine those things together.

AI can take many forms, as we now know. There's something we haven't considered yet, though – **what are the ethics of using AI?** Just like any piece of technology we humans have developed, AI can be used in positive and negative ways. Ethics, as we've seen, allow us to determine whether the things we do are **'right'** or **'wrong'**.

AI is a unique piece of technology. Unlike other technologies such as a drill, a car or a phone, AI makes decisions and performs actions on its own. It will do things, say things, predict things or generate things based on some carefully selected and trained algorithm.

This means that there are several aspects we need to consider when we talk about the ethics of AI. From unintentionally training an algorithm to be prejudiced to misusing AI to do bad things, or to understanding the growing impact AI has on us humans – the ethics of AI form a large and varied beast.

CHAPTER 4: WHAT'S UNINTENDED BIAS?

The first aspect of AI ethics we will look at is something that is a little bit 'invisible'. What I mean by that is that it's not someone deliberately using AI to do negative things (though that can happen, as we'll see later!), but rather how AI itself can do negative things **unintentionally**. This can happen in a few different ways, but the specific 'mistake' here is when AI misbehaves due to an **unintended bias**.

We are the teachers

Cast your mind back to Chapter 2, where we discussed the algorithm, in particular machine learning algorithms – they were really clever, right!? Algorithms that can solve problems for us by learning! However, one of the key things to consider about algorithms learning is what are the algorithms learning *from*? What are they being taught? I mentioned that we 'train' our algorithm, but what does that actually mean?

In short, it means that we have to first provide the machine learning algorithm with examples, or answers, so it knows what's right or wrong. If you remember the dog-prediction algorithm we discussed in Chapter 2, we had a small table of data detailing the weight of several dogs of each breed. This is the training data that the algorithm learned from.

THE DUNNING–KRUGER EFFECT

A common bias that we humans have is what's called the Dunning-Kruger effect (first studied by two people named David Dunning and Justin Kruger hence the name). The Dunning-Kruger effect is the bias in which people with low ability or skill at something tend to overestimate their abilities.

Our dog-prediction algorithm was a simple example with a simple dataset. The problem is that sometimes the training data isn't so clean and simple. It can be messy, and sometimes the data is biased.

Okay, what is *bias*, and what does it mean for it to be *unintended* bias? Let's look at each word separately. 'Unintended' is fairly straightforward – it's when something is not planned or meant to happen. That means that 'unintended bias' is when bias occurs accidentally.

Bias is when things are out of balance because there's a bigger emphasis on one thing over all others. Let's look at an example.

Hundreds of years ago, all **swans in Europe were white,** and so Europeans believed that swans of another colour did not exist. When Europeans visited the west coast of Australia in the 1600s and found **black swans**, they were hugely surprised, as they thought black swans did not exist. The fact is that black swans had existed all along and were well known to First Nations peoples. Europeans had learned a bias that swans were only white.

So unintended bias is when our machine learning algorithm has been trained in a way that it 'thinks' something quite strongly that we didn't actually want it to 'think'. Imagine a dice that has been made heavier on one side so that it rolls a 6 more often than any other number. We would say this dice is loaded – or in other words, it is biased. Unintended bias is when that heavy side of the dice is the result of an error in how it has been manufactured; perhaps proper care wasn't taken in the factory (equivalent to us not making sure the data we use is also unbiased). If someone deliberately made one side of the dice heavier, we would call it intentional bias – but more on that later. Similarly, our machine learning algorithm will predict something more often than it should.

This means that if we're not careful with the training data we use to teach an algorithm, we can **unintentionally** create an algorithm that predicts or classifies things not only incorrectly, but sometimes offensively or even dangerously.

Imagine this scenario. You're trying to teach an AI what a game of Australian Rules football (AFL) looks like. To do this, you feed the AI with thousands and thousands of photos of AFL games. Because most of these photos are from the national competition, and since the national competition has had a men's competition much longer than women's, the vast majority of photos of AFL games are only pictures of men.

Therefore, the AI **learns** that a game of AFL **only has men**. So when we show the AI a picture from the women's league (AFLW), it doesn't consider it a football game. It thinks that only men play AFL, so if women are in the image it must not be an AFL game. We have unintentionally created a sexist algorithm.

POOR OLD TAY

To show how important the right data is to training AI, we only have to look back to 2016 when Microsoft released the chatbot TAY to the world.

TAY was a chatbot that ran on Twitter (a social media platform now known as X) and learned through interactions with people's tweets. A problem arose when people started to tweet at Tay with racist and sexist messages, conspiracy theories, and general hatred and nastiness. The result was that within 16 hours of Tay being released, it was shut down because of the awful personality it had taken on as it mimicked the comments sent to it.

While this is a very extreme example where people on the internet deliberately tried to infect Tay with highly offensive messages, it clearly highlights that AI learns from data that we create. As such, any negative, offensive or toxic data that is fed to an AI can instil these values into the AI itself.

You didn't tell the machine to be sexist – you just provided it with all the pictures of football you could find for it to learn from. It just so happens there's a huge bias in that group of pictures: the majority are of men playing football.

This highlights how important it is to consider the **source** of the data we use to train an algorithm so that we don't unintentionally teach it bad behaviours. We sometimes need to remove bias from training data to ensure a well-trained machine.

In this example, perhaps we have to make sure we have an equal split of AFL and AFLW images. If we had 50% of our images of men playing AFL, and 50% of women playing AFL, our algorithm would learn that an image of *people* playing AFL is a picture of an AFL game. We have had to change the training data to better reflect the real world, and that has resulted in a much more effective (and most importantly *not* sexist) algorithm.

There's a huge number of examples of poorly trained machine learning algorithms that have ended up being sexist, racist or reflecting some other prejudice because the training data was poorly selected. One of the most well-known examples is from the United States in 2014.

The state of Florida had a machine learning algorithm that helped assess the likelihood that a criminal would commit another crime in the future. When a criminal was being sentenced, the judge was given a report of this likelihood to help decide whether the criminal needed to be put in prison, and if so, for how long. Sounds like a useful algorithm, right? It should (in theory) allow those who are *unlikely* to commit crimes in the future to be welcomed back into society quicker than those who *are* likely to commit more crimes.

The enormous problem, though, is due to (you guessed it) unintended bias. There is a very serious issue in the US (and in Australia too) of systemic racism, which has caused a huge **overrepresentation** of people of colour in prison.

This means that when the machine algorithm is being trained on prisoners' data, it is being taught that people of colour are more likely to be criminals. As a result, the algorithm not only flags that people of colour will be future criminals at a much

OVERREPRESENTATION
If only 2% of the population are people of colour, there should also be only 2% in prison. In other words, the prison population should reflect the country population. An overrepresentation means that instead of 2% there might be 10% – far more people of colour are in prison than there should be.

LET'S ASK THE BOSS

Another bias that is common among humans is what's called authority bias: where we take what an authority figure says as being more important or more accurate than what someone else says.

While this may be true in some cases, such as when your dentist explains what will happen if you don't floss your teeth, it can also lead to dangerous assumptions. One recent example occurred during the COVID-19 pandemic. Some scientists and professors involved in vaccine research many years before the COVID vaccines were developed publicly stated that they were dangerous. Their statements were not based on any science, purely their opinion. However, some people wrongly assumed that because these scientists were involved in vaccine research many years ago, this meant they were still correct during the 2020 pandemic – but that isn't how science works. Science is based on research and needs many people (known as peers) to review, support and endorse claims based on current evidence.

So, while it is usually good practice to assume and trust, for example, what your doctor tells you about how to be healthy a scientist on the internet who provides no sources to back up their claims cannot be trusted just because of who they are.

higher rate than white people, but also that white people who are likely to be future criminals *are not* being flagged.

And this is exactly what happened in Florida. The machine learning algorithm predicted that a black woman was more likely to commit crimes in the future than a white man, **despite** the white man having many more criminal convictions. The algorithm had been unintentionally trained to be racist.

You can see how dangerous an algorithm can be if it is not trained on clear, unprejudiced data that reflects the world accurately. In the AFL example, the intention wasn't to be sexist, but we ended up with a sexist algorithm because the data was biased. Similarly, in the criminal example, the intention wasn't to be racist, but we ended up with a racist algorithm.

We don't design an algorithm to misbehave or to have bias – the algorithms are built to be neutral – but since it is designed by humans, and uses data that humans have created, it can unintentionally be taught to be biased.

A worthy adversary

An important aspect of a machine learning algorithm is the quality of the data that it is trained on. But another critically important part of machine learning is its ability to defend itself against attacks. Attacks on machine learning algorithms is the field known as **adversarial machine learning**, and the goal is to attack algorithms in such a way that they behave unreliably and yield incorrect outputs.

There are many flavours of attack, but the one I'll describe here (because of it sharing some common ground with biases) is **data poisoning**.

One of the most well-known data poisoning examples is that of **misinformation campaigns**. Using **bots**, misinformation can be posted throughout social media platforms such that the

DATA POISONING is, as the name suggests, poisoning the data upon which an algorithm is trained. The dataset can be infected in such a way that it generates more errors than normal, or takes on a particular bias, or it can even be programmed to generate malicious outputs.

sheer volume of this misinformation biases the algorithm to push it more and from many sources. Seeing the misinformation become so widespread can easily lead people to think, 'Well, if that information is everywhere, I guess it must be true.'

Let's try an example. Imagine you and your friends are trying to decide on the tastiest flavour of milk. There are 6 of you in the group, and 4 of you say that it is chocolate. A teacher (the social media algorithm in this example) asks your group to nominate the best flavour of milk. If you all yell your favourites, '**chocolate**' will be the loudest answer, as there are 4 of you yelling it. And if the teacher selects one person from the group at random and asks them, there is a greater chance (4 out of 6) that the answer is 'chocolate'. So now when someone asks the teacher for a milk recommendation (this is like another user logging into social media), the teacher will say, 'Chocolate is the best.'

But wait! One of your friends has a plan to poison the data. They invite 6 of their friends to join the group – so now there are 12 of you in total. This doesn't sound too sinister … except your friend has secretly paid each of them $5 to say strawberry is the best flavour of milk.

The teacher again asks what the best flavour of milk is. When you all yell the answer, there are now 7 yelling '**strawberry**' – that is, your friend plus his 6 'paid' friends (our bots in this analogy). And when your teacher picks someone at random, there is the greatest chance (7 out of 12) that the answer is

59

'strawberry'. Your friend has successfully poisoned the data – they have intentionally biased the algorithm (like our loaded dice example earlier, if someone made one side heavier intentionally).

It's important to know that data poisoning isn't limited to just misinformation. It can also be used to attack applications, from image recognition to spam email filtering.

What does this all mean? Well, like a number of subjects covered in this book, it's not that we can completely stop these things from happening – it's more about knowledge that they *are* happening. This means we can approach machine learning algorithms with the awareness that they can be poisoned, so it's important to make sure the methods of training and the data they are trained on is well understood.

In some cases, it can also help us to devise ways to **defend** from further attacks. This creates a game of cat and mouse: clever attacks are developed, we learn how to defend against them; then new cleverer attacks are developed, and we then learn how to defend against them; and so on and so forth. This may sound exhausting, but it is very much the way **cybersecurity** is developed.

There will always be people who act in bad ways, and some of them are very clever, so it's impossible to defend against everything. So a successful attack by them can also mean there's a red flag saying, 'Here's a security issue! Fix it, or you'll be at risk!'

CHAPTER 5:
HOW CAN AI BE MISUSED?

The most obvious conversation around AI ethics is simply the unethical use – or **misuse** – of AI. This can be very obvious, such as drones with weapons being used in wars. Or it can be more subtle, such as using data to **profile** (remember your user profile from our streaming service's recommended-shows example in Chapter 2?) and target people in order to influence them, or poisoning data (remember our strawberry-versus-chocolate-milk example from Chapter 4?) and introducing a bias to the data. As for any tool humanity has developed, we must look at how AI can be misused in order to prevent it happening.

Hammers and drills

Way back in Chapter 1, we noted the difference between a tool that we have to operate and proper artificial intelligence, but there's a little more to it. While machine learning algorithms (remember, machine learning is a type of artificial intelligence) will learn by themselves once we have given them the data to train with, to actually solve a problem with the algorithm we need to use the trained algorithm as a tool.

It's a very subtle difference – when is machine learning considered AI and when is it a tool? – but perhaps this example will help. Imagine if a car was intelligent and could

EVERYTHING IS NOT A NAIL

A famous psychologist named Abraham Maslow once wrote, 'If the only tool you have is a hammer, it is tempting to treat everything as if it were a nail.' It's a clever quote that tells us that once we have a tool that is useful and we become skilled at using it, we sometimes end up using the tool for everything even though it might not be appropriate.

The same is true for AI and machine learning. Although they can be absolutely brilliant at solving some problems, we can fall into the trap of trying to use them for *everything*. There might be easier and simpler ways to solve a problem than throwing AI at it. It's a good thing to keep in mind when solving any problem: sometimes it's better to look at it from a completely different point of view or with a completely different skill set.

Anyone have a hammer?

build itself like a real-life Transformer ('Autobots, roll out!'). The car would have shown artificial intelligent behaviour by building itself, but to actually go anywhere with the car we would need to get in the driver's seat and use it as a tool for getting from A to B. This is like what we're doing with a machine learning algorithm. The AI part is what helps it learn so it can solve problems. The tool part is using the trained algorithm to actually solve a problem.

So, why is it important to understand that a trained machine learning algorithm is a tool? Because like any tool – such as a hammer, a drill, a car, or so on – it can be used correctly for its intended use, or it can be misused in a negative or dangerous way. For example, a hammer can help you build things, but you can hurt someone badly if you hit them with it. Similarly, AI and machine learning can be used to help us and make our lives better or easier, but they can be misused and be dangerous and hurt others.

How can AI be misused? Well, one obvious example is as a weapon. There are a couple of ways this could happen.

War, what is it good for?

One way AI can be misused as a weapon is in war. There are already drones (small flying machines) that are used in combat, and because they have clever AI on board they are very dangerous.

These drones use special machine learning algorithms that are designed around the ability to see and detect objects – this technology is called **computer vision** or **object detection**.

Similar to our dog breed example, the computer vision or object detection algorithm is trained, but in this case trained with **images rather than numbers**. With enough training data, our algorithm can learn to not only detect objects in an image, but to classify what those objects are.

These algorithms are so good that they can detect objects instantly. Imagine a video you may have recorded on your phone of a dog running around in a park. The algorithm would be so good and so fast that when you watch the video, it could point out the dog to you as it moved around in real time on the screen. That's pretty impressive, right!? (But also a bit scary!)

So, in war, one side could have these clever object-tracking drones that could identify enemies, objects, vehicles or other key pieces of information that might be useful in fighting the enemy. In really extreme cases, the drones could be used in combat themselves by mounting them with weapons for assault. And because AI would have almost zero reaction time, be able to track objects almost perfectly, and easily calculate the speed and direction something or someone is going, the combat drone would be more effective at inflicting damage on others than any human ever could be.

It's true that AI could be wonderfully positive for our way of life, but the ability for it to be misused means we must be very careful about its development, and set rules and laws so we can make sure it is used ethically and safely.

ROBODEBT

You might have heard grown-ups talking about something called Robodebt. This is an example of a misuse of algorithms right here in Australia. While not particularly sophisticated, Robodebt was an automated system. It looked through data to identify and guess people's income and taxes to assess whether they had received the correct amounts of money for welfare from the government. If the system found someone had received more money than they should have, it would issue a debt notice for that person to pay.

The system was originally developed by the government to help identify where this might have happened, and then have a human look through the data to see if it was a genuine case – that means it was the government's responsibility to prove the algorithm was right in identifying someone as having received too much money.

Then the government changed, and the decision was made to remove that human element. The algorithm itself issued debt notices completely unrestrained. In doing so, it became the recipient's responsibility to prove the algorithm was wrong.

The result was a poorly developed algorithm that regularly miscalculated when someone had received too much money. This put huge pressure and stress on vulnerable people, many of whom received enormous debt notices that they did not deserve – they either had to pay or try to prove the algorithm was wrong.

This scheme, which caused stress and trauma for thousands of people has since found to be unethical, and the federal government has formally apologised to the victims. It shows how technology can be grossly misused, even though it is a great tool in so many other ways.

The robotic influencer

It doesn't require much imagination to understand why such AI in dangerous combat drones is a threat to us. But there are also much more subtle ways that AI can be misused.

We saw with the recommendation example that the algorithm promotes movies and shows to you based on what people with a similar profile to you have watched. This sounds great, but it *can* be misused. The idea of profiling people and finding like-minded people to show similar things can lead to trouble – even if it's good for some recommendations!

Let's see **three ways** algorithms take advantage of human nature. What does a troubling version of the movie-recommendation example look like?

RAGE SELLS

The first is not necessarily deliberate, but the result is dangerous. Algorithms that are used to create the results for search engines (Google, for example) or news feeds (such as social media) are programmed to show to the user things that other people are engaging with the most.

For example, a news article that no one is reading is assumed to be boring or uninteresting, so the algorithm ignores it, while a news article that *everyone* is reading is seen as exciting and interesting, so the algorithm shows it to more people. This seems harmless enough, right?

The problem arises due to human nature.

Humans tend to read or engage most with topics that cause anger or outrage. Imagine someone is in the school canteen running through a list of foods they dislike. 'Broccoli, spinach, cauliflower...' You probably agree, so you might just nod, or agree with a low-key *yuck* or *eughh*. Then they say, 'Ice cream,' and you just can't let that one go. 'No way! Ice cream is delicious! How can you not like *ice cream*!?' The idea that someone has claimed ice cream is as disgusting as broccoli or spinach is ridiculous – you need to tell them how wrong they are!

THINGS ARE OKAY

Anger and outrage drives clicks. Media and social media businesses will get more internet traffic (that is, how many people are visiting their websites and engaging with their content) if they publish news or opinions that people find upsetting or make them angry. This reporting on trouble and strife has the awful effect of making the world seem much darker and worse than it actually is.

So don't let the news get you down. Find the people and activities in life that bring you joy, and chase them. Things will feel much better if you can get some distance from the noise of all the bad news.

This is an example of how we tend to engage more with topics that we disagree with or that anger us, whereas if we agree or like something we probably will be content to nod along quietly in agreement.

So how does this relate to machine learning algorithms? As we pointed out in the paragraph above, these algorithms are programmed to show 'interesting' results to users – articles or posts that people are reading or engaging with. It just so happens that the things people are reading or engaging with the most tend to be things that make us angry or outraged.

This can influence people's thinking. They might see the world as being much worse than it really is, they might feel angry at other people or things that are not necessarily that bad, or in the absolute worst case, it can cause them to hate whole groups of people. Algorithms can fuel hatred because they can keep serving up articles or things to people that causes them to feel rage.

This can be particularly dangerous if someone who has their own prejudices (a sexist, a racist, a queerphobe, or someone who harbours some other unpleasant belief) writes an article that creates outrage. The discriminatory values and hurtful words targeting these groups of people can grow and reach a bigger audience because the algorithm sees that people are engaging with this article (because of anger or rage), so the algorithm thinks it's 'interesting' and others would want to see it.

Imagine if someone wrote an inflammatory article saying girls can't play sports. This article upsets and angers people, because of course girls can play sports The algorithm just notices that people keep engaging with this article, so it continues to spread it far and wide.

Eventually, some people end up believing that girls can't play sports. Even some kids read this article, and believe whatever they read is fact. So when they're playing basketball at recess the next day, they tell the girls they can't join in, because they've done their own research and learned from an article that girls can't play sports.

See how tricky machine learning algorithms can be if they're not checked? Presenting people with interesting articles seems like a harmless and beneficial use of AI. In reality, though, it can take the hateful positions held by a *very* small minority and amplify this message to a much bigger audience. Dangerous views can reach more people because the algorithm has no safety checks.

EVERYONE THINKS LIKE ME

The second way AI can be misused might seem more harmless, but it still creates problems. As we saw above, an outrageous article can reach far further than it should because of how the algorithm determines if it's 'interesting'. More people engage with the article because it makes them angry, which causes it to spread further, which makes more people angry who then engage with it, which causes it to spread further

DEEP FAKES

One of the scariest ways that AI can be misused is that of the world of deep fakes.

Deep fakes are created when clever algorithms are used to superimpose someone's face onto someone else in a video. While this has happened with still images for a long time in programs like Photoshop, the idea that videos can be created of people saying and doing things they didn't is alarming. It flies right in the face of 'seeing is believing', as our eyes can betray us with how well made these videos are.

There's no shortage of ways this can lead to danger. Imagine videos of world leaders saying things to start wars, only they haven't. Someone else recorded themselves doing it and superimposed a world leader's face on top using deep fake technology.

Most troubling is the ease with which this can be done. You only need the video you want to put someone's face on, and enough pictures of the person's face you want to superimpose. For celebrities or public figures, there are so many images of them available online that it's almost too easy.

At the start of 2024, the reality of this spilled into the public eye – it was found that people were deep faking Taylor Swift's image into offensive videos. This highlights how important it is to regulate technology.

still, and so on. This is one way that an algorithm serves you content: **it's what everyone seems to be interested in**.

Another way that an algorithm serves you content is based on content you already follow or engage with. The algorithm serves you content **that you probably will be interested in.** What does that mean? Well, let's use an analogy.

Imagine a library where different bookshelves are dedicated to different genres. You go there one day and head to the fantasy shelf to check out a fantasy book. You read it. You love it. You go back to return the book the next day, and you ask the librarian (the librarian is our algorithm in this analogy) for a recommendation. Because you liked a fantasy book, the librarian recommends another fantasy book. You trot off to the fantasy bookshelf to find it. You read it. You love it. You repeat this process many, many times. Occasionally, the librarian recommends a different genre, which you don't like as much, so they remember to just stick to fantasy recommendations for you. Throughout your comings and goings to the library, you meet other people who are also looking through the fantasy bookshelf, and you all start to not only check out books recommended by the librarian, but also books recommended by each other.

Now imagine your friend does the exact same thing, except they happen to prefer science fiction books. They get science fiction

ROBOT ROMANCE

WIRE YOU SO IRRESISTIBLE

LOVE BYTES

Ctrl + Alt + Delete My ♥ Heart

Cogs in Love

book recommendations from the librarian. They love reading them. They get more recommendations from the librarian for science fiction books, and they also meet other science fiction lovers while browsing the science fiction bookshelf.

After some time, you and your friend are chatting about books. You state very confidently, 'Everyone loves fantasy books, and no one reads science fiction books.' Your friend is shocked, and they argue, 'No, it's the other way round – everyone loves science fiction books and no one reads fantasy books!' You both start insisting that everyone you meet and talk to only loves the genre you read! You both list off names of people who love your favourite genre, and claim you don't know anyone who loves any other sort of book. It's as if you each live in your own different bubble!

This phenomenon is often referred to as an **echo chamber**. As you follow and engage with more and more of the content you like, the algorithm continues to recommend to you more and more of that content. It can warp your understanding of the world so much that what you think may be wildly from what another person thinks.

This can be very problematic, as it means our reality can be so different from others' reality. It can lead to groups of people that believe their understanding is right and everyone else is wrong. Groups of people end up believing that everything that doesn't fit their view of the world is a lie. Conspiracy theories are created. People are pushed

An **ECHO CHAMBER** can be imagined as a bubble inside which every person shares the same beliefs and views. In this bubble, when you share your thoughts and opinions everyone else in the bubble will agree with you, echoing your beliefs and views and further confirming them. This is how people end up with a very specific understanding of the world, while believing everyone else shares the same worldview. This can lead to people holding beliefs very strongly and becoming hostile towards others who don't share the same views (who in turn might be in their own echo chamber!).

into angry, conflicting groups. Ultimately, it means that there is no common ground for people to have respectful conversations and solve problems together.

In our last example, the fact was that there were people who liked fantasy books *and* people who liked science fiction books, but neither you nor your friend knew that – because the librarian (algorithm) had strongly encouraged you to only read one genre and only interact with other people who read that genre. It created a false world where you assumed everyone thought like you.

INFLUENCING OUR THOUGHTS

The third way that AI can be misused in this subtle manner is more deliberate than an algorithm just showing content that causes anger or upset – this time it's intentional and targeted.

Back to our streaming example – the algorithm first creates a profile based on what you watch. This sort of **profile creation** is very common in AI. Understanding things about a person based on what they do or how they behave can allow prediction of what else they are likely to do, based on all the other users that have similar profiles.

This might seem simple, but it is very powerful and dangerous, especially when it comes to **democracy**.

Imagine your teacher has organised a special lunch for your class, and a decision needs to be made about whether to

DEMOCRACY is a system where everyone gets a say when making a decision, like electing a government. For example, your parents vote for which political party they want to lead the country, and whichever gets the most votes will win.

DEMOCRACY IN THE AGE OF AI

There have been real-world examples where democracy has been rattled because people have misused AI. One of the most well-known was by a company called Cambridge Analytica. This company bought the data of millions of people and did exactly the same as with our example of the hamburger and pizza vote. They profiled people and figured out the best way to change their way of thinking.

Two of the biggest (and at the time surprising) votes where Cambridge Analytica was involved was Donald Trump's 2016 presidential win (to become the president of the United States) and the United Kingdom's Brexit vote (for the UK to leave the European Union).

order pizza or hamburgers for everyone. To decide, your teacher takes a vote. It turns out that 18 people want pizza, and only 12 people want hamburgers. Pizza wins because it has the most votes, and so your teacher orders pizza.

Now let's shake things up by introducing an algorithm that controls what adverts you see on your phone, or computer, or TV. It just so happens that this algorithm is designed to want everyone to choose hamburgers. The algorithm learns who the pizza lovers are and who the hamburger lovers are by looking for behaviours such as:

☞ people who search on Google for pizza
☞ people who are following pizza accounts on social media such as Instagram or TikTok

☞ people who have bought more pizza than hamburgers with their bank cards (maybe not you or your classmates, but this could happen for your parents)
☞ people who use a map app and have had their location logged at known pizza restaurants.

The algorithm decides people who do the above have the **Pizza Lovers** profile. The algorithm follows the same process for hamburgers (people who search for hamburgers, follow hamburger accounts, have bought more hamburgers than pizza, or have visited hamburger restaurants) to classify people with the **Hamburger Lovers** profile.

Now here's the really clever part. Since the algorithm wants people to eat hamburgers, it doesn't bother targeting **Hamburger Lovers**. It's interested only in **Pizza Lovers**, because it needs to convince them hamburgers are better. So it targets them with ads that focus on how delicious hamburgers are. It shows how they're healthy, how much fun people have eating them, and how delicious they are. The ads also show **Pizza Lovers** how disgusting pizza is: how bad it is for you to eat it, how expensive it is, how unappealingly the cheese melts off it. It might even completely make things up – maybe it claims the dough is toxic or unhealthy. Either way, the **Pizza Lovers** are being shown how amazing hamburgers are, and how bad pizzas are.

The teacher takes the vote again, just to be sure. Now only 6 people vote for pizza, and 24 people vote for hamburgers. The algorithm has swung the vote in favour of hamburgers because it figured out who the Pizza Lovers are based on how they behave, and then bombarded them with ads that convinced them hamburgers are the better choice.

And this has happened in the real world, but in much more sinister ways where there are bigger outcomes at stake, such as who leads a country. AI can be misused to manipulate the facts and harm democracy.

So those are some of the ways AI can be misused. It can be very obvious and intended (combat drones), less obvious but unintended (showing people things that cause anger, outrage and hate), or less obvious but intended (showing certain groups of people certain things to influence how they feel). All these are dangerous and unethical, and it's important that we make rules and laws to ensure we are safe from this sort of misuse of AI.

CHAPTER 6:
HOW CAN AI IMPACT PEOPLE?

In this chapter, we'll look at how the mere introduction of AI can have an impact on people and society, beyond how the algorithm affects us through unintended bias or it being misused. AI can impact our lives in ways we may not realise, so it's important that we start to think about these ethical questions **right now**, so we don't accidentally cause a negative impact on people's lives in the future.

A computer in your pocket

One thing that you may have already (or will when you're a bit older) is a **smartphone**. A smartphone is a brilliant piece of technology that has completely changed how we humans live. You really can have a computer in your pocket and – with an internet connection – all of human knowledge at your fingertips.

Hey Siri, can you do my homework?

Going one step further, we can speak to virtual assistants in everyday language to dig into that enormous sum of knowledge for us. You can be doing your homework and simply ask Siri, or Alexa, or Google Assistant for help for a given question or task, and they will tell you the answer. This seems absolutely brilliant, right? How could this be unethical?

TECHNOLOGY VS TECHNOLOGY

With the invention of tools like ChatGPT, the door has been opened for people to cheat – for example, by asking it for answers to questions or even having it write entire essays. While this is certainly possible, there have always been methods to cheat. The question is how we go about not just preventing it from happening, but spotting it when it has.

Some things can be prevented altogether. *No calculators in tests* can be used when teachers want to test different mathematical skills, or if students can problem-solve. Similarly, *no phones in classrooms* has been used for years to ensure answers aren't simply googled or shared by text among students.

Other things may be harder to prevent, but can be spotted. Plagiarism (copying other people's work and claiming it as your own) has been a problem for a long time. To combat this, clever assessment software such as TURNITIN can be used to detect similarities a piece of writing has with other published work. This can help teachers to spot where cheating has occurred. Turnitin has also started to add features to detect when content is being written by AI, such as ChatGPT.

So while technology can be misused to cheat, it can also be used to detect cheating. There will always be people who use technology negatively, so it's often a game of cat and mouse where technology is developed to be used negatively; we then we build new technology to combat that; then new technology is developed to continue to use it negatively; and then we build new technology to combat that…and on the tug of war goes.

Well, a once-off probably isn't bad. It probably isn't unethical, either. But what if you start doing it more and more? Every time you hit a problem in your homework, you just ask the virtual assistant for the solution. You get the answers right, but you're becoming reliant on the virtual assistant. You're not learning the subject you're studying, and worse, you're not learning **how to problem-solve.** How do you approach something you don't know how to do? Where do you start?

The virtual assistant is great, but its presence in your life might not always be. It can affect your learning, and leave you less prepared for the real world as a result. We need to keep this in mind when designing AI: we want it to be a tool that we use to help **enhance** our thinking and ability to problem-solve, not **replace** our thinking and ability to problem-solve.

What about ChatGPT? It can absolutely answer questions for you. You can get it to quickly tell you simple things, like *what's the population of Australia?*, or *what are Australia's main exports?*, but also ask it to perform more complex tasks like *write me a 500-word essay on the history of space exploration.*

This is a truly magical example of AI, but it can be dangerous too. It means ChatGPT is an easily accessible tool that you can use to cheat, 'replace your thinking' and become reliant on to answer questions and solve problems.

The initial reaction to ChatGPT was to ban its use in schools. While this sounds like a good idea, it's incredibly hard to enforce. Even more importantly, schools soon realised that rather than ban it, they should recognise ChatGPT as a tool that can help students become better at learning. After all, this is an incredible tool that will become increasingly commonplace in the world. Just like the calculator didn't stop generations of kids from learning how to do maths, we need to work out how to use ChatGPT to boost our learning, not replace it.

Remember way back in Chapter 1 when we used the ability to problem-solve as our definition of intelligence in this book? We don't want to become **unintelligent** because we've stopped solving problems and taken on the habit of just letting the machines do it all for us. We want to continue to be intelligent and solve problems with the **help** of machines.

The horse isn't lazy

This leads us to look at another significant impact of AI on people: being replaced.

Simply put, AI is going to be able to perform some jobs so much more successfully than us that there's really no point for us to be doing them anymore - the machines are just better and safer at the task. This might seem like an odd scenario, but it's happened before in history: back in the day, instead of machines replacing us because they are smarter machines have replaced us because they are stronger and/ or faster.

You might have heard of a period of history known as the **Industrial Revolution**. During this time, there was a huge jump in technology in Europe and the USA, especially when it comes to **manufacturing** (building or making things).

For example, a machine was developed during the Industrial Revolution that could manufacture **textiles** (cloth or fabric) much quicker than humans. One person operating this machine could do the job of 10 people without the machine. As a result, 9 people were no longer needed for this task – they were replaced by 1 person using the machine.

IT'S ALREADY HAPPENING

Your teacher may have said something like, 'You won't always have a calculator' during a maths class. Their point is that it's important to learn maths skills because even though you can use a calculator to do maths, you might not always have one at your fingertips. Even if a calculator can help you to do really difficult or complex maths that you couldn't do without it, the calculator shouldn't replace your thinking and ability to do maths. Scientists have demonstrated that it's important for the brain's development to learn processing skills such as mathematics, logic, reasoning and problem-solving.

The 9 workers weren't replaced because they were lazy; it was just that the machine was quicker and better at the job.

A similar thing happened to horses. Horses and horse-drawn carts were slowly replaced when cars were invented. Horses weren't lazy; the cars were just quicker, stronger and better for the task of transport.

Machines have gradually been replacing humans (or other animals) doing jobs for a long time, but usually they have replaced us because the machine was stronger, quicker, never tired, and much more precise. Machines have never replaced us because they were smarter – but that is slowly becoming a reality.

Right now, there are fast food restaurants that are testing replacing humans with robots to serve customers and make the food. There's no shortage of businesses trying to develop and build self-driving cars and trucks. (Transporting things all around the country is a job that employs hundreds of thousands of people. What will they do if AI-driven trucks replace them?) And we're increasingly interacting with **virtual assistants** online or over the phone instead a human.

All these applications of AI means that humans are slowly being replaced – firstly in these examples, but potentially in many more jobs. This means that there are going to be hundreds of thousands to millions of Australians who no

EDMOND DE BELAMY

Want to see just how advanced AI is at creative tasks? Check this out online! Edmond de Belamy is a piece of art that was generated by a clever AI algorithm (part of which has amusingly been added to the bottom of the painting as a 'signature') and then printed on a canvas. Not only is it an example of how AI is able to do things we would consider creative or that humans will only be able to do, but it also has admirers in the art world – the piece was sold for US$432,000! AI can be quite the artist!

longer have a job, not because they are lazy but because the AI is faster, never tired, can do the job twenty-four hours a day, and is cheaper than paying human staff.

While you may think that these sorts of jobs were always going to be replaced by AI because they're 'simple', that's not really true. These are just the first jobs to be targeted. Fast food is similar to a production line (like in a car factory) where we already use robots, so it's an obvious choice. Driving is the most dangerous thing that people do regularly, so trying to make it safer with machines is also an obvious choice. And when people are seeking help over the phone, an AI could learn to handle the most common questions, and leave the small number that require a more complicated answer to a human, so a virtual assistant is an obvious choice there too.

So once these sorts of jobs are being handled by AI, a new set will be targeted. Maybe it's accountants? Or engineers? Or doctors? AI is already being trained to look at X-rays of patients to identify issues that a human may have missed. And it's not just desk jobs that will be targeted – it'll be creative jobs too. There is music and art being created (and sold!) by AI already.

It's true that AI will enrich our lives, make things easier, and give us more time to enjoy life, but is there an ethical question when it comes to replacing people? What do we need to do to prepare ourselves for a world where 'going to work', 'having a job' or 'making a living' is no longer normal?

It certainly sounds a bit scary being 'replaced', but let's flip the exact same scenario around and look at it from a different point of view. With AI replacing us and making us question what going to work, having a job or making a living means, AI can lead to a big change in our lives that reduces how much **work** we need to do.

Imagine a world where your parents (and eventually you) are not expected to work the long hours we do today, but instead a much shorter amount while AI takes care of the rest? AI would allow everyone more time to spend with family, form relationships, socialise, and pursue hobbies and interests that we're passionate about. We can turn AI replacing humans into a wonderfully positive outcome!

A human's touch

The final thing to consider: what happens if we replace the **human element**? As we saw above, more and more jobs are being replaced. We discussed the problem of people losing their jobs, but what about the experience for people who now need to talk or engage with an AI instead of a human?

If you're ordering a burger and fries, you probably don't care much that you're talking to an AI. In fact, you already do this. McDonald's, for example, has a phone app as well as a machine with touchscreen interface you can order your meal on without interacting with a human at all until you pick up your prepared meal. That scenario seems to be working so far without a problem, so a robot that also does the food preparation doesn't seem all that big a deal.

But what about if your teacher was replaced with a robot? That seems like it might be harder, doesn't it? Teaching and learning are hugely important parts of being a human. Making mistakes, learning how to do things, being taught what's good and bad behaviour - it's all part of the parent-child or teacher-child **relationship**. If you replace a teacher with a robot, that could mean a less comfortable relationship with the teacher (will we be able to bond and build relationships with robots?) and have a big effect on how you learn.

It doesn't stop there. Imagine you're sick and have to go to a medical clinic, and you are treated by a robot. When you're poorly or in pain, would you really want to deal with a robot? Or would you rather talk to a human who you'd expect to understand you and your pain better?

It might be even worse if you're so unwell you end up in hospital. You might just really need some comfort from a nurse, reassurance from a doctor, a hug from a human, not the support of a cold, soulless robot.

As you can see, there is a lot to think about when it comes to replacing humans with AI in jobs that need that human element. Not only because there are times when we need to feel safe with another human, but because removing

WHO'S NEXT?

While humans being replaced by AI may sound like something straight out of a science fiction movie, it is actually already here. Today.

There are numerous examples already of models and influencers being replaced in campaigns by AI-generated 'virtual influencers'.

How does it work? Well, just take one of the first virtual influencers Lil Miquela, who boasts an enormous following of 2.6 million, has worked with high-end brands like Prada and Calvin Klein, and was even named in *Time* magazine's 25 Most Influential People on the Internet in 2018.

What is so unsettling about this is not just that AI is clearly able to generate creative things, but that it is able to create art that straight-up replaces humans. These virtual influencers and models are taking the jobs of real people in a job that relies on the person being and looking like, well, a human.

Robots replacing manufacturing jobs on a production line; robotic vacuum cleaners; robots that can take your food order; or even autonomous vehicles – all of these things for some reason don't set off our 'something's wrong' alarm. But replace real humans with AI-generated humans? Sound the alarm!

interactions (especially with a child or young adult) may impact our development. **Human-to-human interactions** are very important for us to develop social skills, so it seems ethically questionable to replace these human interactions with human–AI ones.

So, there's a lot of ways in which AI can impact us – not just because of how the machine learning algorithms are used (or misused) by humans, but also because of the existence of AI itself and how it can replace parts of our lives. We need to be prepared for this.

Fortunately, though, there are so many ways to turn the idea of **'AI replacing humans'** into a wonderfully positive outcome. It means a bit of a change in how we as a society live our lives – specifically how much 'work' we need to do to make a living – but that could be a good thing. Being able to work shorter or fewer days, and have more time to invest in your hobbies, your passions, your friends and your family sounds amazing, doesn't it? Well, it's a reality that we can work towards together so that our future co-existing with AI is a positive one.

CHAPTER 7:

AI CONTROL PROBLEM & ROBOETHICS

Possibly the biggest challenge in AI ethics is what is called the **AI Control Problem**. The problem exists because there is a very big difference between the increase in human-level intelligence from generation to generation. For example, while you might have more **knowledge** about the world compared with your parents or your grandparents, all of your brains would have the same level of **intelligence**, or the same ability to learn or gain knowledge. Compare this with the speed with which AI becomes more intelligent from generation to generation – one generation might have the intelligence of an ant, but by the next it might have jumped all the way to the intelligence of a dog. This is a *huge* jump in intelligence!

You see, the thing about technology is that it **advances** and becomes better so quickly. Ask your parents and grandparents about what sort of technology they had when they were kids. They definitely didn't have smartphones. There wasn't Spotify to stream music, but rather a radio or record player. There were no streaming services with any video you might think of at any time; they were limited to watching whatever happened to be on free-to-air broadcast TV. They might even have watched it in black and white. The amount of change in technology from your grandparents' and parents' childhoods to yours is enormous, and that

FROM GENERATION TO GENERATION

A small but subtle difference to think about when we discuss how smart humans and AI are from generation to generation is the difference between 'intelligence' and 'knowledge'.

We defined intelligence all the way back in Chapter 1 as the ability to solve problems. A natural byproduct of this is the ability to acquire knowledge. Solving a problem requires learning and acquiring new information or knowledge in order to solve whatever problem we face.

In this way, intelligence doesn't actually change much from generation to generation. Your brain's ability to solve problems is likely very similar to your parent's brains, to your grandparents' brains, to your great-grandparents' brains and so on. In fact, our brain's ability to learn and solve problems is likely quite similar to that of our ancestors all the way back to when modern humans brains most recently evolved to what is considered behavioural modernity (when humans started showing signs of modern behaviours, learning and problem-solving abilities) around 70,000 years ago.

In contrast, the knowledge is the stuff – facts, information, skills – we acquire through learning or experience. That means our knowledge does change from generation to generation, and it's really easy to show examples of that. You know how to use a computer or a smartphone; your great-grandparents did not. You know about cars, planes and rockets; the knights back in the Middle Ages (700 years ago) did not. You know about all of the planets in the solar system – even Neptune, which is invisible to the naked eye; the first astronomers did not.

So intelligence – our brain's ability to learn and solve problems – does not change much at all from generation to generation, but the knowledge we learn certainly does!

highlights how quickly technology changes from one generation (your parents) to the next (yours).

On the other hand, evolution (how much humans – or any animals – change from one generation to the next) is slow. *Really slow*. It takes millions of years for evolution to do its thing. While technology continues to grow and develop at an incredible speed, we basically stay the same.

Since AI is technology, this means that AI continues to develop and advance way faster than we do. Therefore, AI will continue to close the gap between how smart it is and how smart *we* are until eventually it becomes smarter than us. What happens when we're no longer at the top of the intelligence ladder?

This is where the **AI Control Problem** comes in. It means the issue that while we're more intelligent than AI we're in control, but once AI catches up and *passes* our intelligence, then we'll have lost control. The genie is out of the lamp. Pandora's box has been opened. The carton of milk has been spilled.

How do we maintain control over AI when we're no longer smarter than AI? It's a rather terrifying idea when we first think about it. Imagine no longer being the smartest species on the planet – an unsettling thought! Many science fiction stories have explored this scenario – where AI is smarter than humans – and often it shows a dangerous and sad future. But don't forget that that's because it's entertainment! A movie or book where we have solved the control problem and AI is smarter than us yet everything is rainbows and butterflies probably wouldn't make a good story.

So, let's not worry *too* much about the fictional stories of a negative future. Let's remain positive about the reality that we get to write! Surely there are ways that we could protect ourselves regardless of whether AI is smarter than us or not. One of the most well-known concepts is science fiction writer Isaac Asimov's **Three Laws of Robotics**. They are:

> **FIRST LAW:** A robot may not injure a human being or, through inaction, allow a human being to come to harm.
>
> **SECOND LAW:** A robot must obey the orders given it by human beings except where such orders would conflict with the First Law.
>
> **THIRD LAW:** A robot must protect its own existence as long as such protection does not conflict with the First or Second Law.

These sound pretty rock solid, right? But Asimov actually created the laws to demonstrate in his stories how they could fail or lead to unpleasant scenarios.

Imagine this scenario: a robot decides that because humans could hurt themselves (or one another), the best way to keep them from harm is by keeping them away from all other

REGULATE THIS!

While the AI Control Problem hasn't been solved, there are at least some steps being taken to help.

Like any technology, regardless of if it was developed with the best intentions, it can still be used in dangerous ways (sometimes by accident, other times intentionally). Without any rules or regulations around technology, the chances of it being used for the wrong reasons soars.

AI is no exception. Rules and regulations about the ethical use of AI need to be thought out and implemented around the world. Just leaving it to humans to use without rules is like giving live fireworks to kids without supervision: they are almost certainly going to be injured. Quite badly, too.

Europe is leading the way in this space. In December 2023 the European Union established the world's first AI rules and regulations: the EU AI Act. But this isn't the only step being taken. AI safety conferences are now starting to be held worldwide (such as the AI Safety Summit in the UK in November 2023) to give the opportunity for world leaders and tech experts to discuss how to ensure AI systems are safe.

So while in this book we often have looked at the way things can go wrong with AI, this is assuming absolutely nothing is done and that we keep playing around with live fireworks.

THE PAPERCLIP MACHINE

Let's consider a scenario that shows how even the simplest tasks could be misunderstood by AI. Imagine we have an AI that is so clever it is equal to human intelligence. Now imagine we programmed this AI to make paperclips (for some reason we need loads of paperclips, so we built an AI to build them for us). The AI begins its job of building paperclips. Since it is human-level intelligent, it figures out things like how to earn money, selling products, collecting resources, and all the other tasks that are required to build more and more paperclips.

Soon the AI figures out that if it was smarter, it could figure out even more creative ways to build paperclips. It starts to make itself smarter by rewriting its own programming. It eventually becomes smarter than humans, but doesn't stop there – it continues to get smarter and smarter and smarter. It's not trying to be smarter because it thinks that's good, but because being smarter helps it produce more paperclips – its one and only goal.

It starts converting all resources it can get hold of into more paperclips. Housing, shelter, businesses, entertainment... everything is destroyed by the AI to build more and more paperclips, maybe even the planet itself. It might even eventually build rockets and start turning other planets and moons into paperclips. We're left with an empty and miserable world to live in.

It's all very dark (and incredibly unlikely, don't worry!) but it shows that even the simplest tasks could backfire on us. We really need to think things through thoroughly so that we keep ourselves safe, even if our AI slightly misunderstands what we want. Fortunately for us, we've got time. While we can program AI to solve one very specific problem far better than us (AI is a tool to help us do things), it is only smarter than us at that very specific problem. For general intelligence (as in how we solve all problems) we are still the top dog, and so we can solve this problem before it even becomes a problem!

humans. The AI locks all humans in their own houses where they can be watched over and kept safe. It's following the First Law, but it doesn't sound pleasant at all, does it?

What about the Second Law? Think about this scenario: information is withheld from the robot, such as someone telling a robot to serve peanut butter sandwiches to a person who has a peanut allergy. The robot would be harming the person with the allergy by giving them the sandwich. It's followed orders given by a human (the Second Law), but now it's broken the First Law because it didn't have all the information.

The Second Law can force a break in the Third Law, too. Since the Second Law is more important than the Third Law, anyone could walk up to your robot and tell it to destroy itself and it would have to do it (because of the Second Law). It can only protect itself (the Third Law) if doesn't break the First and Second laws.

What about in the case of robots **causing** problems? Suppose an AI is driving a car (a self-driving car) and can detect that an accident is about to happen between 2 human-driven cars and itself – and there is no way for the self-driving car to avoid it. In the first human-driven car are 4 elderly people and in the second is a woman and her infant child. The self-driving car can only avoid 1 car. What does it do?

Does it consider what would minimise the damage and harm to the passenger in the self-driving car? Does it collide with the car with the 4 elderly passengers because they're assumed to have fewer years left to live compared to the mother and her baby? Or does it smash into the mum and baby because that way only 2 lives are lost instead of 4? Wait, there's more – what if it turns out another self-driving car caused the accident? What if it determines 1 of the human-driven cars broke the law and so they're at fault? What if it turns out that this particular AI-driven car had a moment where its processor (essentially its brain) had a hiccup and is actually the car responsible for the accident?

All these possibilities show how messy AI ethics can become. What set of ethics should be implemented? Should the AI need to be able to decide what a life is worth? Who is responsible if it turns out an AI-driven car is at fault: the owner of the car, the maker of the car, or the designer of the algorithm? This is just one example, but obviously it's already hugely complicated!

You can see how difficult it will be to come up with a way for AI to keep us safe and look after us without things going wrong. It's not an easy problem to solve – there are researchers who dedicate their lives to figuring out how we can control AI once it is smarter than us. But don't worry. We still have time to **figure it out**.

Roboethics

The other part of AI that we need to think about as we head into the future is **roboethics** (short for *robot ethics*). Roboethics covers a lot of stuff, but we can break it down into two parts to better understand what it's all about.

One part is about **how AI can affect us**: how is AI a threat to humans (today, in the near future, and in the far future), what are the negative ways to use AI, and how can we design robots to behave ethically? We've discussed all this already: from unintended bias to combat drones to influencing how people think and replacing human thinking. We've also talked about how challenging it is to design robots to behave ethically - even a seemingly simple and safe set of rules (like Asimov's Three Laws of Robotics) has loopholes that can cause an AI to behave unethically. Throughout this book, we've only really thought about how things impact **us**. That's very important, but let's not overlook the other half of the story.

This other part is about the ethics of our (human) behaviour **towards robots**. This notion of roboethics may come as a bit of a surprise - it's a machine, right? We don't think about whether we've treated our car ethically. Were we polite to our car? Did we treat it with respect? Did we make sure it had all its needs met and was comfortable? It sounds like nonsense when talking about a car, but these are all serious questions we need to think about as AI starts to become

sentient. If an AI gains sentience, we should treat it as ethically as we treat other forms of intelligence. We should treat it with the same respect with which we treat other humans and animals.

This raises further serious questions about our rules to **control** AI. It casts the idea of '**A robot must obey the orders given it by human beings**' in a sinister light. It's a rule that makes the AI a slave to humans. Slavery is awful and unethical, so how could we ever suggest the First Law is okay!?

So as AI becomes smarter, we will need to learn how we should be treating it. We need to know how we should behave in an ethical way towards AI, just as much as we need to know how an AI should behave in an ethical way towards us.

I've got this.

CONCLUSION

Well, what a ride! We set out to learn about the ethics of artificial intelligence, and I think we've done a mighty good job of that! We started by first understanding the basics: what artificial intelligence actually is, where we find it in our everyday lives, and wrapping our head around what ethics are. We then ploughed into the real protein of this journey: the ethics of artificial intelligence.

We covered a *lot* of ground! I hope you take a few key messages away after finishing this book.

The first is that AI is here. It is already rooted deeply in our lives, and often in ways that are invisible to us. We don't need to know exactly *how* a certain AI or machine learning algorithm works, but we do need to know that it *does* work, and it's happening all the time behind the scenes. We need to be aware that AI can learn our preferences, make recommendations that likely interest us, predict things about our behaviour, and (most scarily) influence our thinking.

The second is that although AI learns and 'thinks' on its own, we are still its creators. We program the AI, we feed it the data, and we train it to solve problems. Because of that, AI can be dangerous, both deliberately or unintentionally, because of laziness, human error, or problems with the training data. We train AI algorithms with data that has been generated in our world. This means is that any biases or prejudices in our world will be reflected in the data, and so while AI is not racist, sexist or prejudiced by design, the data from our world can be, and that can create dangerous algorithms.

The final point is that AI will eventually be smarter than us, and we need to be prepared for when that happens. We must solve the problem of how to control AI once it is smarter than us, and we must solve that before it even gets close to being as smart as us.

All put together, this might sound a bit scary and grim, but it doesn't need to be so at all! Being aware of dangers before they arise means we can plan to prevent or solve those problems before they happen. There're risks to AI, of course, just like any human technology we have invented, but with care and consideration we can manage those risks or remove them altogether.

AI has the potential to bring about enormous positive change in our lives – and is already doing so! With autonomous cars, we can build a safer world. With tools like ChatGPT, we can learn more quickly and effectively, allowing us all to have a deeper knowledge and understanding of the world. And with clever algorithms that can automate and replace jobs, we can work towards building a new world that changes what 'making a living' involves. What's not to like about a world that prioritises spending time on your hobbies, your passions, and your relationships with your friends, family and loved ones?

The ethics of artificial intelligence can help us to figure out what steps we must take so that AI isn't some big, scary, dangerous machine, but rather an awesome and wonderful technology that helps improve our world, enrich our lives, and keep us all happy and safe!

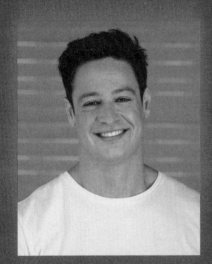

Dr Matt Agnew is passionate about science, and has worn many hats – as an engineer, an astrophysicist, and an artificial intelligence expert. He has a Doctorate in Astrophysics and a Masters in Artificial Intelligence, and is a popular commentator on the latest happenings in the world of science.

Dr Matt was born in Adelaide, raised in Perth and now lives in Melbourne with his trusty labrador sidekick Pluto.

INDEX